T0128284

LEGACY

of

HOPE

ELEANOR WILBANKS

WESTBOW
PRESS®
A DIVISION OF THOMAS NELSON
& ZONDERVAN

This book is a work of non-fiction. Unless otherwise noted, the author and the publisher make no explicit guarantees as to the accuracy of the information contained in this book and in some cases, names of people and places have been altered to protect their privacy.

WestBow Press books may be ordered through booksellers or by contacting:

WestBow Press
A Division of Thomas Nelson & Zondervan
1663 Liberty Drive
Bloomington, IN 47403
www.westbowpress.com
844-714-3454

Scripture quotations are from the Holy Bible, King James Version (Authorized Version). First published in 1611. Quoted from the KJV Classic Reference Bible, Copyright © 1983 by The Zondervan Corporation.

ISBN: 978-1-6642-9263-5 (sc)
ISBN: 978-1-6642-9262-8 (hc)
ISBN: 978-1-6642-9264-2 (e)

Library of Congress Control Number: 2023903446

Print information available on the last page.

WestBow Press rev. date: 02/28/2023

CONTENTS

INTRODUCTION

My name is Eleanor Wirt Wilbanks and I was born on January 25, 1941 to Elmer Augustus Wirt and Willie Pearl Tate Wirt. I grew up in the little town of Arlington, Tennessee. My parents lived on Daddy's stepbrother Aubrey Wilson's farm. I went to school there and I still have many fond memories of the people there and my friends that I grew up with.

I never dreamed that I would write a book but through the encouragement of many special friends, I am thrilled to put my life's story on these pages. I married my husband Edwin L. Wilbanks and we had two amazing girls, Deborah Frances Dunlap and Lori Lynn McDaniel.

A few months ago, Debbie traced the bloodline of our family on both sides. I am asking the Holy Spirit to guide my steps and give me the words that will minister to others as they read these pages. My prayer is that our experiences in life will give you the courage to deal with a situation when tragedy comes your way. As you read about each member of my family, you will know why I chose the title of *Legacy of Hope*.

You go through life and, as you grow older, you begin to think about what you have accomplished. What has your life been all about? Have you accomplished the plans God had for your life and is He pleased? What is your role now as you have gotten older? Will God still be able to use you when you are not as active as you used to be? I think I am starting to get the picture. Yes, He can still use us regardless. I want to reach my generation of ladies and gentlemen who have given up on their God-given talents because of health issues or lack of use.

I know I have been so blessed and God has been so good to me. I love God my Father, Jesus my Savior, and the Holy Spirit. I am praying that each word will be anointed so that others will see the *love of God, our*

Savior Jesus, and the guidance of the Holy Spirit in our daily lives.

As you read the pages of my book, you will see how God has been with me every step of the way. There were times when I thought I could not make it, but that *strong hand* was there and guided me through each storm. I held on to my faith that was passed down from my great-grandmother Nan Whitworth, who I call Granny. You will learn how my Granny spoke life when she said the word, "No."

You will learn about the tragedy that my daddy's side of the family had to overcome, survive, and live through.

I will share about my marriage to Edwin Wilbanks, my high school sweetheart, and how a young couple struggled with some issues but, with God's help, overcame them.

You will also read how Debbie Dunlap, my oldest daughter, lost two children within nineteen months of each other. You will read how Debbie and her husband Con faced their days after such a tragedy.

You will read how Lori McDaniel, my youngest daughter, was impacted when a relationship failed and how she reached out to God for answers. She wrote a letter to God asking him for a husband with certain qualities, and He answered her prayer. She met John McDaniel and they fell in love. They blended a family and started a new business in the very beginning of their marriage.

DEDICATION

I want to dedicate my book to all of the people who have gone through various issues in their lives yet do not seem to understand the *why*, the *how,* and the *what next.*

I also want to dedicate this book to several of my friends who have encouraged me to share my story. I never in my wildest dreams ever thought that *I could* write a book. I realized that we live in a world where people are hurting for various reasons and my story may give them the courage to go on with life. I send a big thanks to all of you who have given me the encouragement to dive into this endeavor.

Cecil Brockwell Carter, my best friend from Bartlett High School, was the first who was instrumental in sharing my story. She told me that I had a story to tell. I am still friends with Cecil but her health is failing, and I want to share what her encouragement has meant to me.

Thank you to all of my friends at Country Gardens, a business owned by John and Lori where I have worked for twenty years. To Janice Rogers Edmiston, one of the employees at Country Gardens, thank you for your encouragement in telling me that my life's story would minister to so many people. Janice is the daughter of the late Reverend Adrian Rogers, minister at Bellevue Baptist Church in Memphis, Tennessee for years. His ministry reached millions of people through his ministries at the church, television broadcasts, and countless speaking engagements in various areas. Janice was the one that named my book *Legacy of Hope*.

To Mary Gracely, an employee at Country Gardens, who was told before she left for her hometown that she had to hear my story. I shared my story with her and with tears in her eyes she told me that *I had to write a book*.

To the other employees at Country Gardens—Judy Westpy, Ginger Porter, Tanya Robinson, Eleanor Ellie

Palazola, and Mikala Speck—thank you for all of the love and support over the years and thinking that my story had to be told.

Thank you to my girls for your support and for telling me you were excited that the Holy Spirit was leading me in this direction.

DEDICATION TO VICTORIA COVINGTON

I have a special dedication to a special young girl that I have grown to love and you will to when you hear her story.

I was trying to come up with an appropriate book cover to be in keeping with the title LEGACY OF HOPE.

I began to research symbols for the word HOPE and I found several listed. The one that caught my eye was a beautiful butterfly. I felt like that would be perfect.

One afternoon I took an afternoon nap and I dropped off into a sound sleep. I had a dream and it was so colorful and vivid that when I woke up I had to stop and think was it a dream or did I see the picture in my dream when I was wide awake.

My mother lived in our home for ten years before she died. She had her own living room, bedroom and bath. When she went to Heaven I moved into her living room and made it my home office, tv room and my own room. She had a sofa and I had it recovered and it happens to be one of my favorite pieces of furniture in my home.

So in my dream I saw a beautiful butterfly that had landed on my mother's sofa. I could not get the dream out of my head. I talked to my daughter Debbie the next morning and shared my butterfly story with her.

She went to a Hair Salon that day and she looked up on the wall and there was a painting with a ladies face that was rested in her hand like she needed some type of comfort and a butterfly had landed on her face. Debbie was overcome with excitement and asked for the artist contact information. When she got home she told me about the artist and about the painting. She was so excited and was anxious for me to get in contact with the artist. I called the number and talked with her mother Jessie Covington about her daughter Victoria. She shared her story and I knew that God led me to contact this family and I called it 'my God winked experience.'".

Jessie said that Victoria was born premature and weighed a little less than two pounds. She lived and suffered all kinds of serious health issues. She was finally diagnosed with Epilepsy and she is in pain so much of the time. She has to spend a lot of time at a hospital for treatments. When she was nine years old she discovered that she could paint and when she was painting she felt a relief from pain. She still paints and does the most beautiful heartfelt paintings.

I also found out that she speaks at various events and shares her story. She has written a book and she is in the process of designing her book cover. I cried and cried and got so excited about how God made it possible for Victoria and her family to become part of my life. I have had visions of the two of us working together for the Lord. When you put the *young with the old* I just feel like we can reach people of all ages that need encouraging. It will show to them that you are never too young or too old to be in service for our *Wonderful Heavenly Father.*

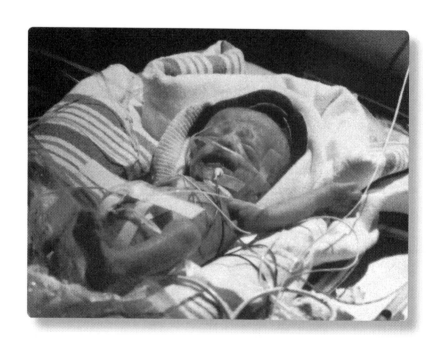

About the artist

Victoria Bradley Covington was born weighing 1lb and 13oz. She was a fighter from birth pulling through heart surgery, blood transfusions, and multiple other procedures in just the first weeks of life. She continues to be seen at multiple specialty clinics for her epilepsy and other illnesses at Arkansas Childrens Hospital. She began painting at nine years old to distract her from her seizures. She says her art is therapy and makes her feel less stressed. Her favorite medium is oil paint. Victoria credits God for her ability to paint. She is homeschooled and enjoys playing with her chickens, cats, birds, and dogs.

MY MOTHER'S STORY

WILLIE PEARL TATE WIRT

In this chapter, I will write about my great-grandmother Nan Timbs Whitworth, who I called Granny. She was married to Clinton Langdon and had two children: a daughter, Willie Frances Langdon Tate, and a son, Clinton Bud Langdon. I do not remember what happened to her first husband or how she met her second husband, Walter Whitworth. They had one daughter, Gladys, and two sons, Hopper and Douglas.

Willie Frances Langdon met and married Jesse Tate, and they had a son named Vernon. Everyone called her Frances. When Vernon was two years old, she got pregnant again.

On May 29, 1921, Frances went into labor. She delivered a little girl who was premature and only weighed three pounds. Frances died after giving birth, leaving a two-year-old son and this precious baby girl. The doctors were notified, and Frances's mother, Nan Whitworth, came as quickly as she could. Immediately, the doctor told her that the baby would not live, being so small and premature. It was unheard of in the community for a baby like this to survive. The doctor said he would take the baby with him. Nan, being a strong Christian woman, told them that her baby was breathing and they were not going to take her anywhere. She, with all her strength, said, "No, you will not take my baby, and *she will live.*"

Nan, who was known as Granny, took the baby home with her and named her Willie Pearl Tate. Immediately, she placed her in the middle of her feather bed and began taking care of that tiny girl. Granny would wrap Pearl up like a burrito and put her in a drawer in her stove to keep her warm. I think the Holy Spirit was leading her in how to take care of this tiny, premature girl. She used her stove like an incubator.

It did not take long before news went out to the community of Poplar Grove, Tennessee about the baby and what Nan was going through. I am sure that prayers went up and people came running to see what they could do for Granny.

Granny stayed by my mother's side, and in fact, she put her head on the side of the bed and slept there night after night, staying as close as she could to this little girl. She tried every kind of milk, and nothing seemed to agree with her. Finally, she tried a very rich milk like Eagle Brand, as it is known today, and that was what agreed with her. The baby lived.

On Willie Pearl's first birthday, Granny brought the community together to celebrate. Granny said that everyone came and brought food and gifts to help celebrate the miracle baby.

I cannot imagine what Willie Pearl's daddy, Jesse Tate, felt losing his wife, and having a premature baby and a two-year-old son. What was the daddy going to do?

Granny took Mother and Vernon to her home and raised them. Jesse had a drinking problem and stayed drunk much of the time. He did not come around too much and left complete responsibility for raising his children to Granny.

Mother was always glad when Christmas came because that was when she was able to see her daddy. I do not remember too much about my granddaddy because he was not close to our family. Mother and Daddy always made it a point to visit with him and see if there was anything he needed. On some of our visits, I could tell he had been drinking. He never could remember my name and called me "Pearl's girl." I felt sorry for him and, as a young child, I thought about the tragedy in his life.

He married again, and Estelle was loved by everyone. They had two sons, named Earsel and Bud. Both of Mother's half-brothers died at an early age, their lives ending in tragic situations.

I heard that Mother's daddy accepted the Lord before he died. There was so much drinking in Mother's family, and she talked about how she knew it had ruined so many of their lives. Her brother Vernon had a sad life; he died at an early age but accepted the Lord before he died. He wrote Mother letters and shared with her his journey with cancer. He shared that someone had talked to him about Jesus and he was so excited because he was saved and knew his final home would be heaven.

Granny and her husband, Walter Whitworth, whom they called Pa, had a good living at that time. He was a farmer and did well for the family. Granny loved to cook and spent much of her time canning fruits and vegetables from her garden. Pa loved my mother and called her "Pa's baby." She said they had a home with nice things, but when Pa died, Granny had to give up her home and took turns living with her children.

Mother loved to tell us about her childhood. She said that she was so grateful to Pa and Granny because they had given her everything in life. Both of them loved her so much. She was proud of them and said they were highly respected people.

Mother loved telling about how Granny loved going to the tent revivals when they came to her community. She was a little Pentecostal lady with a strong faith. Granny loved going to church. She took her daughter Gladys and Mother to Ardmore Baptist Church, which was located in Memphis, Tennessee. Mother was baptized there in 1949.

Mother also talked about a church she went to when she was a little girl of about six years old. It was in Drummonds, Tennessee, in Tipton County. She said it was a beautiful white church with stained glass windows. Her fondest memories were there. She and Gladys walked for three miles through a pasture of cows and bulls to go to church. She would add that the bulls did not scare her.

Granny's love for the family kept them close, and I know she prayed for each one. I know her love for the Lord gave her that determination to make it through each phase of her life.

Mother told me stories about Granny, and I got to spend a lot of time with Granny when she came to visit. As I got older, I thought about this little, thin lady who was very quiet. However, when she spoke, you listened. I knew she loved the Lord, and she spent much time sitting out in the yard reading her Bible in the sunshine. She loved to quote her version of the Bible, saying, "The world will stand a thousand years but not thousands." I never knew what she meant by that phrase.

She also had her own little sayings: "Well, pretty is as pretty does;" "She made her bed and she will just have to lie in it;" and "A bird in a hand is worth two in a bush." I think about those sayings, and I think about her a lot.

Granny taught me in her own way about the love of the Lord and the importance of going to church. I loved to walk down to the Baptist church not too far from my house. I accepted the Lord at a young age. I remember hearing the song "I Believe." The song says, "Every time I hear a newborn baby cry, touch a leaf, or see the sky, then I know why I believe." I knew the words of that song were powerful, and if everyone took them to heart, there would not be a lost person on earth. When I was young, I lived in Arlington, which was very far from Memphis. Somehow, I ordered that sheet music and read over those words repeatedly. I still love that song, and I know what an impact it has had on my life.

Mother would often wonder what her mother was like, and she missed not knowing her. Even though she was loved by her grandparents and they spoiled her rotten, she longed to know all about her mother.

Back in those days, so many families had married children living with them, and they shared chores. Granny liked to cook, and Daisy, who was married to Granny's son Clinton, liked to clean. She told me that Daisy and Clinton treated her like she was fragile and did not let her do anything. They still kept her warm even when the weather was getting warmer. She said they just about burned her up. I have the cutest picture of her wearing leggings and a sweater. Even though there was so much love in her family, she at times felt like not having her mother made her feel like something was missing. It was. There is nothing like a *mother's love.*

I heard a message about *speaking life into existence.* That message changed my life, and I learned the importance and the power of what is in the tongue. As I listened to the words of the minister, I thought back to the words my granny spoke: *"No, you are not taking my baby, and she will live."* That brought life to my family, and there is more to come as I tell my story. Just remember, and place in your heart what Granny's words did for my mother and how God honored those very words. Positive words can do so much for you, including bringing life.

I have always loved the book of Genesis, especially where God talks about the creation of man and woman after He spoke the world into existence.

> So God created man in *His own image,* in the image and likeness of God He created him, male and female, He created them. (Genesis 1:27 NKJV; emphasis added)

If we are created in *His image* and He spoke the world into existence, then what power do we have in our tongues? I learned this message early in my life and I passed it on down to my children.

I often refer to my glass being half-full. If life hands you a lemon, make lemonade. Yes, we can do it.

This is a message I pray that everyone takes to heart. Life and death are in the power of the tongue. Stay positive and pass it down through the generations that God is love and we are created in *His image.*

I taught my girls the importance of this way of life.

MY DADDY'S STORY

ELMER AUGUSTUS WIRT

My grandmother Virginia "Virgie" Funk Wirt was born and raised in Arlington, Tennessee. She met and married her husband William Wirt. On December 27, 1908, she had twin boys and named them Elmer Augustus and Ernest Aurora.

Her story is quite different. I recently have learned more about just how hard her life was. My daughter Debbie has researched the ancestry of both sides of my family. We have learned about the heartbreaking situations my grandmother Maw had to live through.

Her grandparents came to the United States from

Germany and could not speak any English. Her mother and daddy were farmers. I think she had a good life. When her boys were five years old, their father William Arora was murdered. He was shot and killed while living in Memphis. The police did not find out who murdered him. If they did, we never learned anything about it.

My grandmother did not have any means of supporting herself and her boys. She moved back home with her parents, who lived close to Arlington. I do not know much about those years of her life. When her boys were ten years old, she married John Wilson from Arlington, Tennessee. His wife had died, leaving him with five children. He owned a beautiful home and I remember going to the house when I was a little girl. Virgie, known as Maw to me, did not know what was ahead of her when she entered into this marriage. The story I heard is that there was not room in the house for Daddy and his brother so they had to live in a barn or a shed at the back of the house. They did not have the right kind of clothes to wear. I am not sure about any other situations they had to endure. I have recently learned that Maw did all the cooking, laundry, and all of the chores of keeping up the big house and taking care of the five children. I also learned that she was not allowed to sit at the table with John and his children. She had to stand and wait on them until they finished eating. Then I guess she was able to eat and make sure her sons ate their meals.

As I remember Maw, I wish I had known some of the things she had to go through in life. I would have shown her so much love with hugs, and asked her to tell me more about her family and her childhood. I can remember her not smiling very much and seemed to be sad so much of the time. However, being young I did not really know what to do to add more to her life.

Daddy was a very kind, loving, and forgiving man. Daddy told me that when his step-daddy was on his deathbed, he looked at my daddy and said, "Son can you forgive me for the way I have treated you?" Daddy said yes. I do not know when that was, but I imagine it was after Daddy left home and then came back to be with his mother. His words taught me the importance of forgiving. Those words rang true when I had to face forgiving someone later in my life.

I always loved to hear the stories about his life after he left home at a young age. He and his brother left home when they were no older than fourteen. As the story goes, Daddy caught a ride to Mobile, Alabama with some folks who came through Arlington. He lived with them and managed to earn his own living. I never heard about his life from the time he left home until he came back to Arlington. I remember that Uncle Ernest, Daddy's twin brother, moved to California.

I remember my daddy so vividly as a little girl. I remember how handsome I thought he was and how he was a sharp dresser. I remember him telling the story of how he came back to Arlington and met my mother. They married when he was twenty-seven and she was sixteen.

My daddy wanted to live close to his mother and he tried to visit with her as often as he could. Even though he was not raised with her during part of his life, I think he knew how hard her life was. He understood and wanted to show her a son's love. In fact, I think he saw her and visited with her the day she died.

I do not ever remember having a meal with her

during the holidays, but every once in a while she had me spend the night with her. We slept in her feather bed. She always wanted me to write a note that she sent to my Uncle Ernest, who still lived in California. I saw him one time, and then again, when he came home for Daddy's funeral. I have such fond memories of him during his visits.

Maw loved her camera and every time I went to visit her, she wanted to take my picture. She would have me pose and hold my hand a certain way. She would smile when I got in the right position. I heard a click and there was another picture of me.

I do not know if Maw accepted the Lord or not. I cannot remember anything about her spiritual life. I do know that Will, her first husband and my granddaddy, was buried at the Gratitude Church not too far from Arlington. I believe that she and her family must have had a part in that church and she may have grown up there. I just wish I had asked her more about her life.

I know that when John Wilson died, her step-son Frasier and his wife Elizabeth came to live in the house with her. Elizabeth was a member of the Presbyterian

Church in Arlington and she took me to church with her many times when I was growing up.

Debbie, my oldest daughter, has studied the history of the Funk family and the Wirt family. Daddy's mother's Funk family history has been very interesting. She found out that Annie Funk, who was born April 12, 1874, was the first woman missionary who went abroad. She went to Janjgir Mennonite Church (Champa) in Chhattisgarh, India and spent time teaching young girls. She was trying to get home because she had received a message that her mother was sick. She was able to get passage on the *Titanic*. When the crew found out the ship was in trouble, they went to Annie's room, told her to pack and immediately, and come up on deck. She was able to get the last seat on the rescue boat. When she settled on the rescue boat, she heard a mother crying for her children. Her amazing love for others caused her to tell the woman to take her seat on the rescue boat. She returned to the *Titanic* and died when it went under. She died on April 15, 1912 on the *Titanic*.

I was so glad to read about Maw's family and I hope she knew what fine people they were. They were members of a certain Christian group called the Mennonites. Some were bishops and others wrote and published music. In fact, they believed that children should be taught music, and they established music instruction in schools and homes. The Funks have written many books and books have been written about them. Debbie has acquired a good selection of their books.

They still own publishing companies and copyrights on new and old music. They own book publishing companies. Their descendants still carry on their love for writing and music. I often wondered where my love for music came from and this is it: the Funk ancestors.

THE LIFE I SHARED
WITH MY PARENTS

Having been being raised without one of their parents, both of my parents wanted to have children. Mother's first baby was born dead and that had a huge impact on them. Mother told me it was a little girl with red hair. Daddy wanted to wait four more years, and then I was born on January 25, 1941. They doted on me and spoiled me rotten. Mother said she could not even leave a room where I was because I would cry after her or my daddy. They struggled to make a living but I never knew we were poor because I was so loved. Four years later, my brother James Ronald Wirt was born. I called him Bubba when I was younger but switched to calling him Ronnie as we got older. My parents lived for their two children and they loved us so much. As I mentioned before, I did not realize that we were poor because both of my parents had so much pride. When we started school, Mother got us five outfits, one for each day of school. I look back on those beautiful plaid dresses for me and the nice shirts and pants for Ronnie. That was the routine each year before school started. We boarded a bus at Arlington, went to Memphis, and shopped until mother had picked out those outfits. I often wondered how long she had to save in order to buy those clothes.

Maw was still living when Ronnie was born. At that time, we were living in Memphis. She came to stay with me when Mother went to the hospital to have my little brother. I was so excited and wanted to sleep in his baby bed before they got home. I remember Maw waking me up the next morning and telling me to get out of his bed because they were walking up the sidewalk. I got out of his bed, looked out the window, and saw Mother holding that little bundle in her arms, wrapped so tightly in a blanket. I could not wait to get a look at him. He was the cutest little boy with red hair and little chubby cheeks. As he grew older, his hair became curly and he had the prettiest curls all over his head. Mother and I went to the store and when we returned, Daddy had cut his hair and all of the curls were gone.

I cannot remember if Mother cried but she sure let Daddy know that she did not like what he had done. During this time in our lives, we moved to Arlington, Tennessee.

He was a curious little boy who noticed everything and asked a lot of questions. When Granny visited, he watched her every move. He knew there were certain things she liked to do. She liked to dip her snuff and sit out in the yard. Ronnie always made sure she had a spit can and he grinned when he got it for her. We all knew that she liked chocolate candy, and loved to fish, dip her snuff, and read her Bible. He got so much joy watching her every move.

He grew up and was a very smart businessman. He married young and had three children.

After a failed relationship, he met and married Geri, and they had a great marriage. She loved him and they spent several happy years together. The years that they shared together at times were filled with sadness due to problems with his children. I cannot tell you that his life was filled with total happiness, but we shared many good times because our mother kept the family together. She loved to have big family dinners and wanted to have her children and grandchildren over at every opportunity.

Ronnie went to be with the Lord in November 2021 and Geri is still trying to make it without her best buddy, friend, and partner. I do know that he loved me and I loved him. As Ronnie got older and his health was failing him, he did not like to get out much. I tried to visit with him but he always said he did not feel like going anywhere and it was not easy for us to get together.

One night, I was driving home from work and something told me to call my brother. He answered the phone and we said, "Love you Ronnie" and "Love you Sissy" and other sweet words. After a few minutes, I could tell he was finished talking so I told him goodbye. Geri came into the room and saw that he was off the phone. He told her he did not feel well, and then he dropped his head and died. What if I had not obeyed that little voice that prompted me to call him? He died five minutes after he hung up the phone.

I thank the Lord all of the time for those cherished words we shared that night. I do know for sure that Ronnie had accepted the Lord.

He told me many times that he had read the Bible all the way through and that he prayed. Geri confirmed how much he loved his relationship with Jesus. I wanted the assurance of knowing how he stood with his salvation, so I wrote him a letter sharing my heart and my love for him. He talked to me and assured me that he was saved. Sometimes words on a page can mean so much to others. Geri said he kept my letter close to him and read it often. He had a dynamic personality that would keep you laughing. He was quite a charmer and he would make you feel like you were the most important person in the world. He started his own business and it was successful for many years.

My daddy loved his son and he loved for them to go fishing together. If Ronnie did not go, I went with

Daddy because I could never tell him no. I still think back on the time we spent together. I learned to fish, to clean the fish, and to fry them. We loved to have our fish fry dinners and invite folks over to enjoy the catch of the day.

I remember going to church with Mother and Granny as a little girl but I never knew of my daddy going with us.

My daddy came in the house one day and told my mother that was almost killed when he was painting the house. He said his hand brushed up against a naked wire and it knocked him off the ladder. He came into the house and told Mother about his narrow escape. He said that is why everybody needs to go to church. You never know what the day may bring.

God heard his plea, and a few months later, Daddy accepted the Lord. I went to church with the Hampton family. They had raised a dynamic preacher who came to the Baptist Church in Arlington to hold a revival. David Hampton and his friend visited people and told them to come to the revival. David Hampton saw Daddy get out of his car after work and met him in the yard.

They shook hands and introduced themselves. David asked Daddy the question that is the most important one you can ask. He said, "Mr. Wirt, "If you were to die tonight, would you go to *heaven or hell?*"

Daddy said, "You know, I have been thinking about that and I want to be saved." He accepted the Lord right there in the yard and went to the revival that week. He loved going to church, and six months later he went to Heaven.

Daddy was only fifty-five when he died. He had a massive heart attack at Firestone, where he worked on Saturday, and died instantly. I was young and it was such a tragic time in my life. I had two small girls who loved their granddaddy so much. My mother was left a widow at the age of forty-four. She later married Leonard Lackey, a fine man, and they were married for nineteen years. When Leonard died, she married another wonderful man, Durrell Carter, but he died after five years of marriage. She was widowed three times but she always managed to get back on her feet. She had that spirit that Granny passed down, and an attitude of that she could make it.

Being a good person, like my daddy, does not get you into Heaven. Accepting Jesus Christ as the Savior is the only way.

> For God so loved the world that He gave
> His only begotten Son that who so ever
> believes in Him shall not perish but have
> eternal life. (John 3:16 NKJV)

MY LIFE

ELEANOR PEARL WIRT WILBANKS

As I sit here thinking over my life, I ask myself, *Where do I begin?*

I am eighty-one and had to think about why I am writing this book. One reason is I want to bring encouragement to all who have a need. All can learn something from my family's tragedies that have left a *legacy of hope* down through the years. I want to provide an answer to some of the valleys that we go through in this life and how to endure them.

I had a wonderful childhood and grew up with much love. I often said that I was God's pet because I had been given so much. I did not have wealth or fame but a good life and so many happy times and great memories.

I have had a great career path. I am still working and love the fact that I can still work. I was hired in 1964 to work at the local bank in Arlington. I went into real estate in 1970. I had the opportunity to work at FedEx in 1982. I worked there for eighteen years, then retired and went back into real estate. My youngest daughter married John McDaniel in 2002. He was in the process of buying Country Gardens at the Agricenter. I was able to help them open and start their new business. I tried to sell real estate and help them too. However, after my stroke in 2009, my doctor told me to choose one or the other. I chose to continue helping them and it has been one of the most rewarding of my jobs. I have been able to watch how those two built a successful business. We have been in business for twenty-one years and the business has been successful. John and Lori have built a wonderful, customer-focused business. It continues to bring in the best plants and products that bring joy and happiness to their customers.

Now I think I will begin my personal journey. I will

explain how I got my name and why my parents named me Pearl after my mother. Daddy loved Mother's name Pearl. He wanted her to name me Eleanor Pearl. Janice Rogers Edmiston asked me to research the story about the pearl. I did my research and this is what I found.

> A natural pearl (often called an Oriental pearl) forms when an irritant that works its way into a particular species of oyster, mussel, or clam. As a defense mechanism, the mollusk secretes a fluid to coat the irritant. Layer upon layer of this coating is deposited on the irritant until a lustrous pearl is formed.[1]

My interpretation of this is that when an irritant works its way into your life, your only defense mechanism is to *give it to Jesus.* He coats our lives with *His amazing grace and mercy* until we become vessels formed to carry on the message of His *faith, love and hope* and tell others what God can do in their lives. You can become a shining

---

[1] "A Diamond and a Pearl," Invitation Ministries, posted March 15, 2022, https://www.invitationministries.com/post/a-diamond-and-a-pearl.

light and a precious jewel to help other people see Jesus in your life and they will want to know Him.

I hope that reading about some of the valleys God has brought me through will be a blessing to you. I think as you read these pages, you saw how my family had to deal with early deaths, murder, hard marriages, and other trying times. Through it all, one little lady passed down *strong faith* that flowed through her family.

I have had a wonderful life and I do not have anything to complain about.

I met Edwin Wilbanks at Bartlett High School. My best friend Cecil introduced me to him and he asked me out. After a few dates, he took me home with him and I met his parents, Lee and Ethel Wilbanks. Their home was filled with a wonderful atmosphere. They were a Christian family and church was a big part of their lives

Ethel was a good cook and I loved the meals that I was invited to share with them. I immediately fell in love with his parents and his sister Mary Frances.

Mary married Al Richardson and they had three wonderful children: Keith, Wes, and Darla. Ed and I were blessed because they loved us and liked to spend time with us. Wes and Darla are still in the ministry. Wes's son Parker is also in the ministry. Keith and his family are Christians. This shows how living a Christian life can flow down through the family.

Ed quit school and joined the Air Force. I still spent time with his family while he was gone.

Ed soon left for his basic training. After the training, he was stationed in Smyrna, Tennessee. We still dated. Being that close to home, he was able to come home on the weekends. At times, he hitchhiked or got a ride with a friend. Somehow he was able to get a car.

Ed wanted us to get married and keep it a secret. I married Ed in 1958; we were young and we were so in love. That was the plan we had until he could afford for me to move to the air force base with him. We eloped on Christmas Day and went to Marion Ark and got married. We thought our secret was safe and he could save some money for me to make the move to be with him. However, his uncle had a friend who read it in the local paper. His uncle shared the news and we were reminded that we weren't too smart after all.

Since all of the family knew about our marriage,

we made plans for me to move to the air force base in Smyrna with him. We bought a small, almost new eight foot by thirty foot mobile home from some good friends. We made the move and managed to get our tiny home to a trailer park right outside of Smyrna. We had trouble but finally were situated and started our lives together.

I met a lady across the street from where we lived, and went to visit with her one day. She started telling me she was pregnant and some of the symptoms she was having.

I went home and told Ed about our talk. I told him I was having some of those symptoms. The look on his face was one of not knowing what to say. As it turned out, I was pregnant. I had an easy pregnancy, but Ed had morning sickness for months. I gained twenty-five pounds and he lost twenty-five pounds. I felt so sorry for him. People started telling him how to keep from having this sickness every morning. None of the advice that he received worked.

We made plans for me to come home to have my baby. Ed took time off and moved me in with my parents for a few months so Mother could help me with the new baby. I was going to the naval base in Millington for the birth and for the remaining check-ups until the birth. The doctors determined I had the Rh-negative factor, which caused additional doctor visits.

Ed's uncle offered him a car since our car was not going to make it much longer. Ed kept hoping that I would have the baby and then he could get the car before he had to report back to the base. We waited and waited. He knew time was running out and he had to make the trip.

He and his mother left for Oklahoma early in the morning to get the car. He had only been gone a few hours when I went into labor. Mother was cooking turnip greens and Daddy kept telling us that we had better get to the hospital. I waited until I had eaten her turnip greens and corn bread, and then we left. The trip to the hospital was not a good one because my labor pains were getting harder by the minute. I think every time she hit a bump in the road made it worse.

Our first daughter was born on November 8, ten and a half months after we got married. Ed's daddy called Ed in Oklahoma and told him he had a little girl. Ed had thought it would be a boy but was anxious to get back home and meet his little girl.

Debbie was a beautiful little girl and Ed and I realized what the love of a child could be like. He had wanted a boy but when he laid eyes on this little girl, that wish vanished. We named her Deborah Frances and there are so many memories of her. She was a special little girl and walked, talked, and was toilet trained at a very young age. In our small mobile home, she could pull up a chair and reach the sink. She wanted to wash dishes, wash clothes, and do what I did on a daily basis. She loved to do those things all through her life at home and now at her own home. She knows how to make her home very inviting and it is beautifully decorated. She loves anything that reminds her of her family.

Ed took his responsibility of being a young married man with a child very seriously. Debbie had sensitive skin and her diapers had to be rinsed several times to make sure there was not any detergent left in them. He loved to do that for his little girl and he kept plenty of groceries at home for our family. I did not know many people there, so I guess I treated Debbie like a grown up.

Ed sold Bibles and worked at the NCO club to make extra money. He worked hard in order to buy her all the necessary things. He had worked enough to buy her a potty chair and a high chair. He came home from work and wanted to go right then to buy those items. We went into Nashville to make the purchases and he was so proud. The next day, I got a message that he went into the hospital with pneumonia. He had literally made himself sick with all of the extra work. He was determined to provide for the needs of his little girl.

We wanted to have another baby before he got out of the service because we did not know what the job situation would be like. I got pregnant with our second child and we were so excited. Ed thought maybe this one would be a boy. I came home to live with my parents again because it was close to the time for Ed to get out of the service and start his civilian life.

Our baby was due in the middle of July, but I kept saying that I was going to have her on Ed's birthday, August 2, and I did. Our second baby was born and it was another little girl. We named her Lori Lynn. She was also gorgeous and looked exactly like her daddy.

We were still living with my parents. My mother and daddy were such a help with my girls since they were twenty-one months apart. They were a joy and all of the family just thought they had hung the moon.

Ed got a job at DuPont just a few weeks after he got out of the service. He continued to take his responsibility for his family very seriously. My parents bought us a lot next door to them and we were able to build a new home. We bought new furniture and Ed bought a new car. We could not believe how blessed we were to get such a great start in our civilian life back in Arlington, Tennessee.

Daddy was so in love with my girls and he came every afternoon to see them. He delighted in taking them to the store and letting them buy candy or whatever they wanted within reason. They loved him. Even though they were young when he died, they still remember him and often share their memories. Children know when they are loved and it is easy for them to retain such happy moments spent with their loved ones.

One part of my story that I have not shared is about Ed's battle with alcohol. I found out soon after we were married that he loved to go out and drink with his Air

Force buddies. The whole time we dated, he did not drink around me except for one time. He knew it upset me so he did not drink around me again. When I moved to be with him after we got married, I found out what his life had been about. Needless to say, I was an unhappy young wife. However, I had to draw a line down the middle on a piece of paper. I had to title one side the *bad* on other side the *good*. I started adding to the list and the good side won out. He continued to drink and I think he wanted to quit but the alcohol had taken hold of him. This went on for years. I grew up knowing what alcohol could do to a family. I did not want us to face some of the issues that alcoholism can cause.

I got a job and I told him I was going to leave because I did not want to raise my children in this atmosphere. He had gotten off work one morning after working the midnight shift. He stopped by a local joint and starting drinking. He said he noticed an old man at a table close to him who had his head on the table. He was lying in his own vomit. As he looked closer, he realized that he was a young man. He said the Lord told him that his life was headed that way if he did not quit drinking. Praise the Lord he got up from the table and the Lord sobered him up. He quit drinking after that because he wanted to raise our girls and give them the right home life. The Lord got his attention and life was good.

We raised our girls in church, and our home was always filled with friends, music, and laughter. Ed and I sang in a gospel group for years. I still remember his testimony about how the Lord got his attention about drinking. He was able to share that he was an alcoholic, and after his encounter with the Lord, he was able stop drinking immediately.

We loved every minute of our days with some of the greatest people on earth. We put together a group called the Good Time Gospel Singers. We had Kathy Frasier on the piano, Leon Moss singing tenor, and Donnie Ashton playing bass. Ed sang the lead and Leon and I swapped the alto and tenor parts. Leon was a fine Christian man and it broke our hearts when he died at an early age. Donnie started with us when he was fourteen and stayed at our home much of the time. He is still in our lives and he is like our son. In fact, he calls me Mama and Ed Ditty. We have maintained a relationship with Kathy and we share so many great memories. I have cherished memories of those days with people who were like our family. Some of my memories were our trip to Atlanta to make a recording. At that time, London Paris had formed his own group, London Paris and the Apostles. I do not remember all of the details, but one of his singers had become friends with Kathy. He arranged for us to go to the studio in Birmingham and record an album. I still love to hear those songs today.

I also want to tell you about a young friend of both my girls and how she came to live with our family. Her name is Kathy Paris Steen, the daughter of London Paris. She met my girls and they became best friends. In fact, she was instrumental in getting them to attend First Assembly Church on Highland in Memphis, Tennessee. She was instrumental in getting them involved with the youth ministry there. She has been with us all of these years and has been there for us through death and the good times.

Her family is like my family and I refer to her as my oldest daughter. She lost both of her parents because they both died at an early age.

We enjoyed our days of singing for various occasions. We remained in church, enjoyed our friends, and continued to fellowship with Christian friends.

Ed loved to spend time with his girls. He bought a boat and taught both of the girls how to ski. He enjoyed taking their friends to the lake and showing them all a good time. Life was good and filled with so many friends and so many good times with them all.

You know how the devil wants to destroy the family. He comes in and tries to destroy you through your weaknesses. When Lori turned eighteen, Ed started spending a lot of time at the lake and he loved to fish. I think he must have thought, *I have raised my girls and now it is my time.* I guess you would call it a mid-life crisis.

He was around people who loved to drink and his life spun out of control. He started drinking again. We had been married for twenty-five years. I was devastated that he wanted to fish all of the time and that he had started drinking again. Lori was still living at home and I did not want to leave her every weekend by herself.

I never enjoyed being around a lot of drinking since I

was a young girl. Too many in my family loved to drink and I never liked that atmosphere.

I tried to spend my time going to church and shared in all of the family events. Some friends I had known for years, Terry and Judy Graves, were singing with a gospel group called the Seekers. They felt they needed to spend more time with their children and wanted the group to find someone to take their places. They recommended me and I auditioned with the group. Stan Kesler, the sound engineer for Sam Phillips, told them I was not country enough. They told him they were trying to put together a gospel group not a country group. They voted me in and I started singing with them. They also added Danny Smith as lead singer right after that. We had a good sound and I have so many wonderful memories of how the Lord blessed and anointed our group. We practiced at the Sam Phillips studio and I spent almost two years with them. I still cherish their friendship and cherish the memories we shared.

The group included Gary and Sheila Climer. Gary played saxophone and Sheila sang alto. She also could sing a solo that had people sitting on the edges of their seats. J. M. Vaneaton was the drummer and he became the drummer for Sun Records studio when he was around sixteen years old. In fact, he is still being recognized as the great drummer he is and for all of the records that he recorded with famous groups. Danny Smith was our lead singer with such a great anointing. Stan Kesler was our sound engineer. Stan Neil played the most beautiful guitar and he could make it talk. Wendell Lee played the piano with a great sound and Jim Stockton played that walking bass style. Stan Neil, Stan Kesler, and Wendel Lee have all gone to be with the Lord. I loved bringing a little harmony to the group and still love to talk about the great times we had in ministering to so many local churches. We went to churches in Mississippi to sing. We participated in local events. I am still good friends with all of these wonderful folks.

Our weekends were filled with Ed fishing and me singing. Our marriage was on the back burner and we drifted farther and farther apart. I look back and wonder what should have been done to save our marriage. Nevertheless, after twenty-five years of marriage, we were divorced.

I loved my family and, even though my girls were grown, I prayed that God would restore my family. It was a hard day when I found out that I was divorced and twenty-five years had ended this way. God did hear my prayer and He restored my family. Ed and I reconciled and married for the second time. Both my girls were prayer warriors and they were happy we put our family back together.

I was working at FedEx. We made our marriage work, but I had spent so much time by myself while he was away fishing and drinking. Both of us had things to work on. At that time, I was determined to make things work. Ed had so many wonderful qualities and I had to focus on the good times.

I went back to drawing a line down a page and listed the good and the bad. The good won out again.

Ed and I built a home, and added a living room, bedroom, and private bath so my mother could live with us. She had been widowed three times. We were so close and I wanted her to enjoy her life.

She loved to dust, clean house, and do laundry. She liked for me to cook, clean floors, and the other chores we had to do to maintain a good home. She loved her family, her grandchildren, and her great-grandchildren. She loved it when they all came to see her and let her know how much they loved her. She told people much she enjoyed her visits with them,

She was also a caregiver; she showed how to make someone feel comforted. I remember how she helped me take care of my girls when they were newborns. They loved her so much.

MY JOURNEY WITH CANCER

In the early 1980s, I went for my yearly checkup and my doctor found some blood when she took a stool test. She sent me for a colonoscopy and I really did not think much about it. When it was over, the nurse told me to go to the doctor's office. When I walked in, the atmosphere in the office made me wonder what the doctor was going to say. He said, "I will know more when the test comes back, but I think you have colon cancer."

The words rang out and I said, "*Cancer?*" The news upset my mother, my husband, my children, and my church family. I had surgery and a year of chemotherapy, and I had such good care. After a few months on the weekly chemo treatments, I got sick. My immune system had broken down and I had to go to the hospital. My family, my church family, my friends, and my FedEx family all rallied around me.

My director at FedEx, Eric Freeman, came to visit with me. He made me an appointment with Dr. Richard Wanderman and I began treatments with him to help build my immune system. His treatments pulled me through. I had to finish my chemo. All of the ones who stood with me were still providing me with their support. They helped me to get through that tough year and the precious Lord and Savior was there with me every step of the way. When you think you just can't make it, *He shows up and tells you that you can.*

THE DEATH OF MY MOTHER

On September 18, 2000, I had planned a big day with my mother. I was going to take her for her yearly mammogram. I had some errands to run and one of them was to do some banking. Then we were going home for lunch. After that, she wanted to go shopping again to find a birthday gift for her daughter-in-law Geri.

On the way to the hospital for our first stop, Mother was in deep conversation. She asked me what I thought about the death penalty. I told her I would have to give that some thought. The night before, we had gone shopping at Macy's in search for some gifts that Mother needed. It was the routine and, if she got tired, she would meet me in the shoe department. I saw her sitting there with a beautiful black couple and an adorable little boy sitting in his stroller. Mother was telling his parents how amazing he was. As we were leaving, she told me that he was so precious and if she could have, she would have brought him home with her. We laughed and you could tell she really enjoyed her visit with the family.

We passed by Bartlett Baptist Church in Bartlett, Tennessee and she asked me how Rodney Dunn and his wife Valerie were doing. Rodney was the associate pastor and Valerie led the women's ministry. She loved Rodney and it upset her when I told her that he was no longer at the church. She had been a member there for years and, when she met Rodney, he became special to her.

We finished at the hospital and I ran one more errand. The next stop was Peoples Bank to make a deposit for me and cash a check for her.

When we came to the parking lot, it seemed dark and dreary and I did not have a good feeling. Usually I went through the drive-in window, but everyone would ask about her so I asked her if she wanted to go in to see some of the employees. She was quiet for a few minutes and then said she wanted to go in. I can still remember the look on her face because she hesitated to say yes.

We went in and the manager was in his office. He saw her and asked us to come in to see him. They entered into a big conversation, so I left his office and went up to the teller window to do my banking. The teller was still working on a transaction from the customer before me and she sounded confused. She apologized for taking so much time and I told her to take her time. I knew she was trying to straighten out something before she could wait on me. She took my deposit, and I heard my mother telling me not to forget to cash her check. I did not turn around to answer her because I was still trying to let the teller take care of her work. I just nodded my head.

All of a sudden, I heard this horrible sound and, out of the corner of my eye, I saw a large man with a gun jumping over the counter. I was immediately alarmed and I think my blood pressure went through the roof. I turned and it felt like I was walking in air. I did not know where to turn or what to do. I backed into a room and then I thought about the safety of my mother. I thought the manager would know what to do and how to keep her safe. I heard her call my name and then I heard a shot. I knew the robber was yelling at the teller and I thought he had shot her.

All of a sudden, it became quiet and I heard the manager on the phone. He was calling 911 and telling them that a lady had been shot. I thought the robber had shot the teller. Then I heard him say that an elderly lady had been shot. I cannot tell you all of the emotions that I went through at that moment. I stood there in complete shock, not knowing what to do. The next minute a police officer arrived and led me out the front door.

I saw my mother lying between the doors with her

head surrounded by blood. I could tell by the way she fell it must have been an instant death. Later, I found out that she did die instantly and probably did not know what had hit her.

My mind went through so many emotions when I saw her there on the floor. I felt fear and was horror-stricken but yet also felt a moment of peace. I later realized that the moment of peace was because she had entered into Heaven. Mother had made so many comments to me about her death. She told me not to cry when she died because she had lived a long, good life and God had been good to her. She also indicated that she did not want to live to be eighty-something years old. She was so comical in some of her thoughts. She would say, "I don't want people looking down at me and saying, 'Look at all of those wrinkles.'" I asked myself why those thoughts would come to her mind. She would also snap her fingers and tell me that is the way she wanted God to take her. So many expressions still go through my mind at times.

After I got through the front door, the officer put me in a car with a lady who was trying to help me get control of myself. She asked whom she should call. I was able to remember the phone numbers and she started making the calls to my family. She told them what had happened and where. I was in such a state that I had to get out of her car and get down on the ground. I thought I was literally going to die. People gathered around me; I was in such a state of shock that I do not remember anything they said to me.

They put me in an ambulance. Two of my friends the lady had called came immediately to the scene. Valerie Dunn and Sandy Roe stayed in the ambulance with me and members of my family begin to arrive. In fact, these friends stayed by my side for days. My youngest daughter Lori had been led to believe that I had been killed. She nearly fainted when she saw me in the ambulance. She then went into hysterics when she realized her grandmother had been killed.

When I got home, so many friends were there taking charge. One called my doctor, who sent me a prescription to help me get through the next days. The television news broadcast the story repeatedly. Helicopters were flying over my home and the schools had been let out early for fear the robbers might be hiding somewhere close. My driveway filled up with news reporters wanting to talk to the family about what happened.

My precious friends were there taking charge in the kitchen and answering phone calls. One called my doctor to tell her what had happened. I heard her say she was sending me a prescription to help me cope. One of the friends said she was almost afraid to give me these meds because it seemed like a lot. I remember thinking I did not care because my heart was about to explode.

One of the news reporters asked for a picture of Mother so the community could see the face of the elderly lady murdered at the age of seventy-nine at the local bank. I thought it had to be a dream. I looked around my home and everything reminded me of my mother and what I had lost. I cannot even begin to tell you what I was going through. My girls, sons-in-law and my grandchildren were all devastated.

When my brother came to the bank, he immediately asked, "Where was the security guard?" Some of the bankers told him that he was out to lunch. We later found out they did not have physical security but had data security on their staff. He had felt like they were not telling him the truth about the whole situation and it bothered him. Of course, he kept his feelings to himself because he was worried about my mental condition.

The next morning I woke up and I could tell there were a lot of people in the breakfast room. I thought I could not face the day and deal with the nightmare that had happened the day before at the bank. I heard a little voice that said, "Yes, you can do it." I had a picture in my mind of my mother and my daddy together. I could see a reunion between them, their first daughter, and mother's mother Frances. At that moment, that image brought me peace.

I made my appearance in the room where all those people were. There were people from the bank and people from the federal court. I don't remember anyone else except family and friends.

Lori and Ed went to the funeral home and made all of the plans for her funeral. They planned to have the funeral at Bartlett Baptist Church.

I suffered the tragic death of my mother and the survivor guilt, not knowing how I would live through this horrible and tragic incident that no one would ever dream could happen.

Again, my family, my church family, my friends, and my doctors were all there to help me. Debbie became the speaker for the family because the news media and the newspapers wanted to hear more about this elderly lady and her love for her family and the Lord. Debbie was so gracious and she kept talking about mother and the Lord. People were drawn to her testimony because she did not show any hate and was only focused on how the family was coping during this tragic time. I would say the bloodline of my granny was present during this time.

Mother had told me that she wanted to join Forest Hill since Rodney was no longer at Bartlett Baptist. She said, "Who would preach my funeral if I died?" She did not need to worry about who was going to preach at her funeral. Three of our favorite ministers preached and it was a wonderful service. Each one of them captured what she and her life were all about.

She immediately got to know Bob Geabhart, our pastor, and his family personally when she joined Forest Hill Community Church. He was one of the ministers who preached at her funeral. Debbie had given Mother a book to write her life story. Debbie gave it to Bob. He read through her writings and said she helped perform her own funeral. Bob has been in our lives for so many years and he is like a son to me. He stayed by my side through the death of my mother, my battle with cancer, and other issues that came my way.

Rodney Dunn, who she loved dearly, also preached her service. Rodney and Valerie spent a lot of time with me during this horrible experience and helped me through many a night when I could not sleep. Valerie would talk to me for hours because I was having horrible flashbacks of that day in the bank. Through the death of my mother, Rodney was inspired to start his own church. It has grown and his oldest son Jonathan Dunn is the head pastor.

My nephew West Richardson also preached at her service. West is still in the ministry. He has been faithful and God has blessed him through his years of ministry.

The music was amazing. My friends Joanne Coscia played the organ and Kathy Swoffard played the piano. Kathy Steen and her daughter Ashley, Dianne Geabhart, and Dave Roe sang with such an anointing and those beautiful songs meant so much to me. Since music had always been such a part of my life, I was able to be at peace during the service. Mother loved music and loved to hear those ministers preach, so I know she was proud.

They spoke about her love for the family and that she was a message that reached the whole community. She kept asking what her role in life was since she was a miracle. People commented that they wanted to be better mothers and love their families like she did.

My whole family were members at Forest Hill Community Church. Debbie was on staff at the church. The church was growing and we were in the process of building a new building. Mother had joined the church and had donated her rings to the building fund. Talk about legacy! Mother had said, "I do not have a lot of money to give to the church for the building fund, but I can give my rings. I want to contribute something as a legacy of how much I appreciate the work of this church."

The Friday before the grand opening service at our church, the men who had robbed the bank were brought to Memphis. The news aired the story that day. Some reporters showed up at the church on Saturday while some of the members were preparing for the service on Sunday. So many of the news media came to the service that day. They reported about the church my mother had joined and said they wanted to be there so they could report on the service. The message that went out about my mother and the church brought new members in, and it was such a blessing to all of us.

My brother and I spent the next five years in the courts. I was told that I needed to hire an attorney so Ronnie and I would know what had happened in the bank that day. We hired Gary Smith and he was with us all through the years to come. My pastor Bob Geabhart was also there with us. When the men were brought to Memphis, the robber who had the gun in his hand that killed my mother wanted Bob to come to the prison. He wanted to explain what had happened that day. He said that the manager was trying to get out the front door. He had told him to lie down in front of teller row but he broke loose and started out the front door. He tried to pull him back in with his right hand

and had the gun in his left hand. The manager pushed his arm back trying to get free, hit the hand with the gun in it, and it caused the gun to go off. Mother was caught between them and the bullet went up through her shoulder, hit the back of her head, and killed her instantly.

The robber did not know that he had killed her until he heard it on the news. He wanted to tell his story. He met with Gary and shared his story with him. He said that he could not sleep without seeing Mother's face before him.

I met with his parents during one of the court hearings and they apologized for their son with tears in their eyes. He had three small children and had moved into a new house. Some of his kinfolks had started this ring that went around robbing banks. This was the first time that this young man had gone with them and he wanted to make some extra money.

At first, the federal court was asking for the death penalty. They changed their minds when they found out more of what had happened in the bank. The men were sentenced to life in prison without the possibility of patrol. I thought back to Mother asking me what I thought about the death penalty.

At their sentencing, the men were sitting in a row at a table. I had to take the stand. Each one of them asked me to forgive him. Mother loved to sit in her chair and write down thoughts that came to her mind. Lori had gone through her papers and found many notes she had written. She also found letters she had written to me and to Ronnie. One note said, "As the Bible says you must forgive in order to be forgiven." I looked at each one of them and I told him that I did *forgive him*. I also remembered that Daddy had forgiven his stepdaddy for how he treated him when he was young. I can truthfully say that I have forgiven them. I go back to the lines my mother had written in her note and what Daddy had told me verbally about *forgiveness*.

I have had so many people ask me, "How did you ever live through that horrible situation?" My only words were that *it was the Lord*. When you know in your heart that God is your Father, Jesus is your Savior, and the Holy Spirit will guide you and be with you, the only thing you can do is to pray and ask for healing and comfort.

My mother always told me not to cry and grieve over her when she died. She was a miracle and she really did not know what her life was all about. She said she had a good life. She said to remember our love and how much of our lives were spent enjoying the family. I immediately began to see the impact that she had on so many people's lives. Her love for her family and her strong willpower taught others that *yes*, they can make it. Debbie had a dream about the reunion Mother had with her mother when she arrived in Heaven. Debbie said she saw her meeting Frances and her little girl that was stillborn. She got to see my daddy again, and oh what a reunion that was. I pray that my mother's life story has helped someone who needed a word of encouragement.

ANOTHER HEALTH ISSUE

After the death of my mother, Ed and I were still having issues in our marriage. Because of these issues, Ed and I divorced for the second time. We had grown farther apart and drinking was still an issue in our marriage. I felt like there was no way we could ever make it together again. Our divorce was final in March 2009.

Debbie asked me if she could invite her daddy home for Father's Day. I told her that I wanted them to have a good relationship and she should invite him to come home and spend some time with her. She called him but he did not answer her call. He called me and wanted to know what she wanted. I told him that she wanted him to come home for Father's Day. I told him that he should come home and that he was welcome. I did not think we should be hostile to each other and we should think about the impact of what divorce does to a family. I told him that we had a guest room and he was welcome to come and be with his girls. He said that was sweet of me and there was a tone in his voice that I had not heard in a while.

He arrived bright and early that Saturday morning. He told me later that if he did not leave early, he may have started drinking again and would not be able to come. He came without bringing anything to drink and God took the desire for alcohol from him again. He will tell you now that he is an alcoholic and wanted no part of that life again. He said he would advise everyone to never take that first drink. You do not want to become an alcoholic on purpose but it can take over your life and take you down an ugly path that is hard to give up. He said, "I wish I had never tasted that first drink and smoked that first cigarette." In his older age, it has caused him some health issues.

I was busy with choir practice at church and really did not see him until Sunday. He let me know he regretted the divorce. Debbie bought him some clothes so he would not go back to the lake. He did not go back to the lake and he kept staying at home. He kept begging me to get married again. I told him I had to be sure that the drinking was over. Debbie never gave up on praying for her daddy and she just knew that God was once again going to restore her family.

In December, Debbie and I went to Lori's next door for breakfast. I started feeling very tired and I told them I was going home. When I got home I started feeling dizzy so I lay on the sofa. The phone rang and when I got up to answer, I could not walk straight. It was Lori and I told her to tell Debbie to come home because I was not feeling well. When Debbie came in, I asked her to give me an aspirin because I thought I was having a mini stroke. She called my doctor and they told her to get me to the hospital. We told Ed that we would let him know what we found out and would call him. We felt he was better off at home. At the hospital, the tests results showed that I had had a stroke.

Debbie or Lori called Ed and told him I had a stroke. He came to the hospital. I could not feed myself because my right hand was affected and he tried to feed me with his shaking hand. I thought, *Now isn't this a pretty sight with two old people that can't even help each other.* I agreed to marry him again. I went home from the hospital and started my healing process. Ed kept talking about getting married again and this time I told him I would marry him again for the third time. He said if we got married before the end of the year, it would mean we would file our tax return as a married couple.

It was early in the day before Christmas Eve and we decided to go to Hernando, Mississippi, where we were married the second time. I was still recuperating from my stroke but I managed to carry on with the plans. When we got to Hernando, they said there was a three-day waiting period they had put into law a few years before. Ed asked where we could go and they said Somerville, Tennessee, which was not too far from our house. He drove there and we got our license. However, they told us that the judges had left early and there was no one there to perform the ceremony. However, they knew a minister we could call. Ed called him and he agreed that we could come to his home. When we walked in, there were Santa Clauses of all kinds around his home. He had a white beard and looked like Santa Claus himself.

I told him I was recovering from a stroke. Since we had been married two times before, I asked if he would sign the license and let us go. He said that he was sick and his wife was on the way home to take him to the hospital. He told me he was going to perform a religious ceremony and we both would make it. I told Ed not to tell the girls about our wedding and especially about Santa Claus. When I tell that story, people start laughing. What can I make out of this story to encourage someone who may need some marriage counseling? I guess that

I would tell that person to do whatever he or she has to do to keep the family together. The main advice that I can give is to allow God to be the head of the household.

I went through physical therapy. Because the stroke affected my right side, I had to learn to write again, I had to gain strength for my balance and my voice was affected. I had so much care from my family and I slept for weeks and weeks. I recovered and there are no signs now that I had a stroke.

I was concerned about my voice because I still loved to sing. I noticed two young girls at church who sang so beautifully and I could tell they were trained. I asked them whom they had taken voice lessons from and they both said Terri Theil. I called her and told her what had happened to my voice. I asked if I could schedule a time to see if she could help me. We set a time and I told her jokingly that if she could not help me, then I would take dancing lessons. I went for my first meeting with Terri. She played the piano and I started singing a song for her. When we finished, she looked up at me and she said, "I think I can help." I started my lessons with her. I cannot tell you how much I enjoyed my time with her.

We spent approximately ten years off and on together. I consider her one of my best friends and we have so many memories to share. Once, she was contacted by a couple from Florida who loved Elvis Presley and wanted to get married in the Elvis Presley Wedding Chapel. She chose me to sing for the wedding and, of course, they chose songs that Elvis had recorded for me to sing.

THE DEATHS OF TWO OF MY GRANDCHILDREN

This will be the most difficult story for me to tell.

Talking about my grandson and granddaughter, who left this world way too young, brings back memories and I end up with tears in my eyes. It has left a hole in all of our hearts and especially those of their father and mother Con and Debbie Dunlap. How do you lose one much less two within nineteen months of each other and survive? They both have a *strong faith and that is the only reason.*

Lauren was a special little girl who loved being with me from the time she was three years old. She loved to spend the weekend with me and Pop. She loved to go food shopping, as she called it, and loved to help me cook dinner.

I loved to go to church with her because, as a young girl, she would sit in the seat next to me and write about the message on a piece of paper. She always had a strong love for Jesus and for what was right about living. At the drop of a hat, she would pray for someone in need. She learned to play the guitar and had a beautiful voice. She loved to minister in worship songs to her Heavenly Father. She was invited to sing for various youth gatherings and you could tell she was born for ministry.

She grew up and moved to Dallas, Texas to go to Christ for the Nation College. There she became involved with the Praise Team under the direction of Klaus Kuehn. She and Kari Jobe were the lead singers. When Lauren began to have trouble with her voice, she stepped out of music and became part of the prayer ministry. At that time, she was engaged to a wonderful young man but broke off their engagement because she did not feel that God meant for them to be together. When Andrew Kuehn found out she was not engaged, he started calling her. The Kuehn, McCabe, and Dunlap families were all close friends for years, beginning when their children were all young. Andrew said he had a crush on Lauren since he was a little boy. They dated, became engaged, and were married.

Andrew was from Michigan and Lauren was living in Dallas. Of course, her parents Con and Debbie were living in Memphis.

They were married in Memphis and moved to Dallas. Right away, Lauren wanted to have children. Her first baby was a gorgeous girl and they named her Lily. Two years later, she had a boy who they named Titus. Two years later, they had another boy named Aiden. Two years later, another boy, Elias, arrived.

Andrew and Lauren had so much in common because they were both amazing worship leaders. When Andrew played the piano and they both sang those beautiful worship songs, you could tell they were anointed to sing for Jesus.

Lauren never missed a chance to come home after her babies were born. She would pack them in the car and head to Memphis. We looked forward to her visits and we were so happy to see those babies.

After Elias was born, Lauren began to have some pain on one side. Debbie went to Dallas to help her with the children. This went on and Lauren finally told someone about the lump she had found in her breast. She did not pay too much attention because she had nursed all of her babies. She decided to talk about it and have a breast exam. I will never forget the day I was driving down the highway and I called Debbie to see if they had found out the results of the test. I could hear the babies crying and Lauren screaming. Debbie told me the news that it was cancer. She said Lauren got in the tub for a bath and felt her ribs breaking. The ambulance was on the way to take her to the hospital. I had that horrible feeling of helplessness sweep over me, so I turned around and went home. I lay on the sofa and could not stop crying. My baby girl had cancer and I could not get over my grief. My little dog Sophie was on the back of the sofa and Ed said, "Look at your dog because she is crying and wiping her eyes." I had rescued her and she rescued me on various occasions; this time she did not leave my side.

I knew Debbie was at the hospital with Lauren and

folks had come quickly to take care of the children. Andrew was devastated and we all could not believe what was happening. I could not hear any news because there were so many people at the hospital. In fact, because Lauren had ministered in so many churches there were ministers who immediately came.

Chase, her brother, called me and said, "Nana, there are so many people praying in the halls and the doctors and nurses are allowing them all to remain there." He would also call and give me updates.

Lauren and Chase were so close growing up and he loved his sister so much. He had also moved to Dallas and started going to college with her. He also lived with her for years and helped her take care of her babies. Those children loved their Uncle Chase. Chase got a good job and wanted to have his own place, so he moved before Elias was born. Chase had helped start a business in Dallas and then he was moved to Austin to start the company there.

Lauren got out of the hospital and was going through treatments in Atlanta at the Cancer Centers of America. We had prayed and we were expecting her to be healed.

Andrew and Lauren moved to Austin, Texas to join Rick Pino's ministry.

Then more tragic news hit our family. We got the news that Chase had been killed in Austin, Texas, where he lived. Ed woke me up early one morning and told me to get up because Chase had died. Here again, this news hit me and I did not know if I could make it. I went into the kitchen and there were my precious Debbie and Con trying to figure out what they needed to do. They had to make the trip to Austin and had to make arrangements for what was to come next. Lauren was making funeral arrangements for her brother who she loved so much. Our family was dealing with more grief and praying for strength for Con and Debbie as they had to face the situation in Austin. Lauren was in the beginning of her battle with cancer, but she had the strength to endure the tragic news about her brother.

Once again, my family and I were facing another tragic death of a young person who died at the age of twenty-eight. Friends and family came to my home and took over anything that needed to be done. Kathy Steen came and wanted to have someone clean our house.

Some of the people she called were not able to come. However, Cheryl Potter, a young lady that I had known since she was born, heard the news and came by. She told me about the cleaning business she had started so she could be home as much as possible with her two boys. She offered to stay with me and do whatever she needed to do to help during this horrible time. She was such a blessing and she has been with me ever since that day. She and her family call me Nana and love to take care of Pop. God is so good and sent the right people at the right time to help us through the tough times.

Meanwhile, Lauren was planning a beautiful celebration of life for Chase at First Assembly on Walnut Grove. Once again, Bob Geabhart was helping our family to have a wonderful service at the church. Chase's uncle Ed McCabe spoke at the service and Andrew and Lauren sang a duet. It was a beautiful service. Chase had met Rick Pino, and loved him and his band members. They all packed up and came to Memphis to play for the service.

Since Lauren was still battling cancer, Con and Debbie moved to Austin to help with the babies. They rented an apartment and Con got a job transfer with FedEx. When Lauren became really sick and Andrew could not work, his daddy offered him a job in Michigan. He told him to come work for him so he could continue to support the family but still be there for Lauren. This was a heartbreaker for Con and Debbie with their sick daughter moving so far away. Nevertheless, they had to understand the situation and take it as best as they could.

The move was hard on Lauren, but she made it and settled in at the home of Andrew's parents. She was able to see an oncologist. Her doctor told her she would do everything she could for her and provide the latest treatments to beat this horrible disease. Debbie, Lori, Kathy, Ashley, and I drove to Michigan to visit with her. When we arrived, she was in the hospital and we had a memorable visit with her.

We spent some time at the Kuehn home and Andrew and Lauren sang for us. We had an anointed service right there in their home. Lily, being just like her mother, prayed for Lauren. She had a bowl of water and she would apply water to Lauren's stomach and ask God to heal her mother. The cancer had moved to her liver and she was experiencing so much pain. Lily knew that was where the pain was. She said she was anointing that area with oil and praying for Lauren to be healed. She had heard me say that my knees were hurting, so she came over to me, put water on my knees, and prayed the sweetest prayer. With her head bowed and with all her heart, she said, "God please heal these old, old knees and make them young again like these other girls." Her words and actions went through the room and her prayer still remains in my heart. The room filled with laughter, but tears were also streaming down many of the faces there.

Lauren was in and out of the hospital for treatments. At one time, we thought she had won the battle. However, the cancer attacked her liver and she did not have the strength to fight. I never gave up hope that she would win the battle and she would be healed. On Christmas day, she died and went to Heaven. How does a parent give up two children whom they loved so much within nineteen months? How does a family go through such a loss? As Debbie would tell you, it was through our strong faith and the comfort that only God can give. She had a beautiful service in Michigan, and another one was held in Dallas. The church that she and Andrew had ministered in was packed. She left a legacy there and we began to see the fruits of her work. So many people began to tell us how she had ministered to them. It has not been easy, and it will be five years this Christmas of 2022. We know that their short lives here on earth made a difference to so many people. Not a day goes by that we don't think about them.

Lauren left four beautiful children and Andrew makes sure that we get to see them often. They fill that void. Con and Debbie know that they want to be strong and help raise those children. I talk to Andrew and we have some deep conversations about the children, his future, and plans for his God-given musical talent. We share our deepest thoughts with each other and I love talking with him.

Andrew wrote a song about Lauren and the words brought tears to our eyes. One of her cousins had a recording of the song on her phone and she played it for some of the people in the room. One of those people happened to have connections with a music studio in Nashville. He loved the song and the testimony about Lauren. The next thing we knew, Andrew was in Nashville recording the song.

Don Ashton, who was such a part of my family, heard the song and Andrew's testimony about Lauren. He made a video, published it, and put it on YouTube. You can watch it on YouTube and I promise you it will bless your heart. The title is "That Sweet Memphis Belle," written by Andrew Kuehn and published by Don Ashton. I encourage you to listen to the song and pray for Andrew and those four children who had to watch their mother suffer with cancer and who had to give her up when they were young.

My heart goes out to families who have lost young children through military service, from drug overdoses, from automobile wrecks, from so many deadly diseases, and from other tragic situations.

OUR GOLDEN YEARS

I know we have had so many things to endure during the past several years. Ed and I both have had some minor health problems. I am so happy that God restored my family and that Ed and I have been together to face the heartbreaking issues our family has experienced. We still live in the home that we built almost thirty years ago, and we are there for each other.

I know that Ed is glad that I shared his battle of addiction. He would tell you to never take that first drink because you may be the one who becomes addicted to alcohol. It is one thing that the devil can use to attack and destroy. I inherited the Funk family Bible from my daddy and which his mother gave to him. It is close to

200 years old. In the middle of the book is a picture of a husband and wife sitting together. Their advice was to never let alcohol be part of your family. Ed also would want you to know that God delivered him immediately twice when he asked Him to take that desire away from him. I have wondered what I did wrong in our marriage. I know that couples can gradually grow apart and one thing after another leads to divorce. I would say keep the romance in your marriage, do a little dating, and talk about the good times. Ed and I have a good life and we tell each other how glad we are that we kept our family together. Our families can say that *we had the help of the Lord* in every trial that we faced.

Our country has gone through a horrible time with the pandemic. I suffered from some health issues that affected my immune system. Ed was also experiencing some health issues. I chose not to get out much and obeyed what the doctors told me to do. I have said that sometimes God allows you to stay still, spend some quality time, and have a closer relationship with Him. I have cherished this time being with my Lord, having those special moments with Him, and listening quietly to hear *His* voice. Every day, my prayer has been, "What do I need to do at this time of my life?" Sometimes we need to slow down and count it a blessing to *be still and know that He is God.*

I never dreamed I would be led to write a book. In my wildest dreams, that never entered my mind until I heard some special people say, "You have got to tell your story." I have enjoyed spending this time sharing my thoughts and going over the things that my family has had to overcome. I hope the legacy of my ancestors and my family will minister to someone as that person reads my book. I also want to express that it is *never too late* to work for the Kingdom. I think my next venture will be to do a recording of all my favorite songs that have ministered to me all through the years. Please help me pray about that.

I pray that in a world full of pain and suffering, we will learn that *God is the answer.* Accepting Him as your Savior will not promise you a life filled with complete peace. I can promise you that a life with Jesus will allow you to have peace in all the storms that come your way. Also, the eternal home that God made for us will be waiting when the battle has been won. God bless you all.

In answer to my question of what I can do at this age, I learn something new every day. I have learned the importance of keeping up with my friends and praying for them. I love to encourage people who need a little help to face the day. I love my family and God has given me my precious girls and their families. I want to allow the Holy Spirit to let me know when someone needs to hear a testimony about *what can bring that person through the trials of life.* I am praying this book will provide for that need for all who read its pages. I am praying that we can all find a closer walk with Jesus and make a difference in our homes, churches, communities, and our country.

I believe we are living in a country in which people think they can do everything on their own and have put God out of their lives. I have news for them: we cannot. I know if we pray we can bring *revival* to a sick world. As I close out the last chapter of my book, I am reading through the pages again. So many emotions are running rampant. I have tears in my eyes, joy in my heart, pride for my family, and a prayer that these words will minister in some way to all who read *my story.*

FROM THE HEART OF LAUREN KEUHN

I cannot close my book without telling you more about my precious granddaughter Lauren Hannah Keuhn. As I write about her, there are no words that can really describe what a special person she was. She died on Christmas Day and it will be five years in 2022.

When I first laid eyes on Lauren, I recognized her beauty and I fell deeply in love with this little girl. She and I had a special bond that was unexplainable.

From the time she was two years old, she loved to spend time with me. I would pick her up after work on Fridays and she would spend the weekend with me and

Poppa. This went on for years. She was not the kind of little girl who wanted to have her nails done, shop for clothes, or do any of the other fun things that I would suggest. She would say, "I want to go food shopping." She would take a piece of paper and make out her list. She would draw pictures of the food items. It was amazing how much the drawings looked like the food and even I could tell what she was describing.

I loved to go to church with her and I loved to watch her enjoy being there. As I remember, she was probably six years old when I noticed she had her Bible open and was making notes of what the pastor was preaching about. She loved the Lord at such an early age.

She also could not watch anything on television that had violence or anything inappropriate. She had high standards that she learned early on in her life and that remained throughout her life.

She loved music and learned to play the guitar as a teenager. She never missed an opportunity to go to worship and sing. She attended college at Christ for the Nation in Dallas, Texas and joined their worship team led by Klaus Kuehn.

She then moved to their prayer ministry and she believed and practiced the power of prayer. Her other talent was being an artist. She loved to paint while someone was speaking. Her work was amazing and it captured a person's heart and story.

Lauren's family had known the Kuehn family for years. Andrew Kuehn lived in Michigan. When he found our Lauren had ended a relationship, he started calling her.

Lauren was still living in Dallas at that time. They fell in love and married. They were both musically talented and began to lead worship. Andrew played the piano and the two of them sang with such an anointing that those who heard felt they had entered Heaven.

Lauren wanted children, and they had one girl and three boys. Lily was her first born, then came the three boys: Titus, Aiden, and Elias.

They were active at a wonder church in Dallas called Shoreline Dallas. Lauren was a member of the sisterhood team at her church. They wrote a thirty-day devotional book and one of the chapters was written by her. I read her message and I thought it was one that we all can use.

I can just see her in Heaven asking all of the ancestors about their lives. She had a contagious laugh and I can imagine her laughing when she got to hear some of Granny's stories. In the following, you will get to see a glimpse of Lauren and her heart.

FROM THE HEART OF LAUREN KUEHN

On Being a Daughter of Promise

"I recently gave birth to my fourth child Elias. Near the end of my pregnancy this amazing thing called "nesting" overtook me. I began cleaning every nook and cranny of my whole house. Every cabinet and closet was cleaned out. My mom came in town to help me with the kids and one evening we were discussing the topic of hoarding things.

"My grandmother was the classic hoarder. When she passed away she had two garages packed from the ceiling to floor of "stuff" that she never had space to use or enjoy. In fact, no one enjoyed it because it was all packed away.

"So many people spend their lifetime accumulating this "stuff" and taking care of it. Only to have it boxed up and kept in a storage unit. At the end of this conversation my decision was clear. I had to end the hoarding madness and after seven trips to Goodwill, was done. I got rid of my random bowls, plates and cups that were ugly, stained and mismatched. I replaced these items with my beautiful china. I wanted to eat every meal served from these special dishes that made me feel like royalty. My family deserves the best! My new mantra is – "Why are we eating off the old chipped plants when we have beautiful china packed up in boxes up in a garage?" We keep thing put away for a "special occasion" to enjoy a few times in our life.

"But the real travesty is so many of us are living our spiritual lives like this. We get so comfortable with our daily routines and we are content with going to church on Sundays; but we have to ask ourselves, are we leaving God there? Like my china, does our special relationship with Christ make us feel like royalty only come out of Sunday or a special occasion like Christmas and Easter? Are we serving our very best in our marriages, relationships and careers? Are we using ugly stained busy-ness and mismatched schedules instead of His best?

"God is ready to invade every part of our lives. Quit settling for mediocrity in your spiritual life. Allow God to come in to every area and have control. In Psalms 21:3 we see how God met David with rich blessings and set a crown of find gold on this head. Only a life submitted to the Lord is truly fulfilling.

"When the Lord delivered the Israelites from Egypt, the appointed time came for them to take the Promised Land that the Lord had ordained for them. Moses their leader sent 12 spies into the land to investigate the situation. Only two of the twelve came back with a good report of hope. The other ten brought back fear of the giants living in the land, warning the risks were too great. The people chose wandering around in the desert with what they knew instead of taking the land that God promised them.

"In what part of our lives are we afraid of taking what God has for us? I am ready to take hold of the land that God has promised me. I am choosing to go after the very best for my family. I am going to press into the heart of my God and submit to Him every circumstance, situation and relationship with prayer and worship.

"Maybe you have been afraid to ask the Lord for certain things. Can I just tell you that our God loves you more than you could ever imagine and he has a Promised Land just for you. He is calling us to not settle with our relationship with Him but to go deeper. Talk to God throughout your day. When you are in a crisis at work, cry out to Him for wisdom. Pray for your co-workers and bless them. God will open up all kinds of opportunities to minister to them. If you are a stay at home mom, invite the presence of the Lord in your home, turn on worship music and let your kids see you worship God. While you are doing dishes, pray with a thankful heart. Let your house be filled with joy instead of a spirit of strife. You have the authority over your home to set the tone for peace or for discord. Take that authority every day. When your husband comes home from work, he will recognize it. Your kids will recognize it. When your friends come over you can pray over them. Use every opportunity God has given you to take the land. Maybe God is calling you to do something that seems out of your reach as He often likes to do because He calls us to do things we can't do without complete dependence up Him.

"I am ready for and am expecting miracles and break thoughts in my life and yours! Let us no longer settle for a mediocre Christianity where Jesus is only talked about at Church. Now is the time that we allow God out of the boxes in our garage and into our every moment."

I always loved listening to Lauren's words that were spoken or written with such passion. I also want to live by her meaning of life. *Give your best to God and live life accomplishing what He has called you to do.*

FROM THE HEART OF CHASE DUNLAP

C hase was a very special little boy and the one thing that he left with us is how much he loved his family and friends. There are so many stories that I could tell you but it would take a hundred more pages.

When he was just a baby, Ed and I loved to keep him. He was so good and I think about the best little boy I have ever known. If he was able to help Poppa with chores around the house, he was happy. He was not a picky eater; he liked to eat and then go for a long nap. He liked being on schedule. He did not want you to make a fuss over him but just let him be.

One day he was working in the yard with Ed. He came to the door with gloves on his hands that he had to struggle to keep on. He had a little raspy voice and he told me, "Poppa and I are hungry. Fix us something to eat." He was probably around three years old but wanted you to think he was a big boy.

Chase loved Lauren so much and they were as close as any two siblings could be. I worked at FedEx and he could remember my phone numbers to call me at work. If Lauren wanted me to pick her up after work, he could call and tell me in that raspy voice that "Yarner wants you to come pick her up." He could not pronounce his Ls so Yarner she became. Any time I moved to a different office, I had to update him with my new phone number.

Chase loved to get out in the neighborhood and meet all of the boys regardless of age. He was hard to keep in the house and would escape at times to visit his friends. He loved to make friends wherever he was. He did not like to be captive and made to be still. Debbie said that he was the only little boy who had ever been kicked out of Sunday School.

Chase loved to work, and he would work harder if you told him how great he was doing. He worked for Country Gardens and then went to Christ for the Nation College. When Lauren and Andrew got married, he lived with them for several years. He lived with them and helped raise the first three babies. Before the fourth one was born, he moved into his own place.

He got a job with the Poop Troops in Dallas, Texas and built that business to become a very successful one. He then moved to Austin, Texas and started the company there; it became as successful as the one in Dallas. He was in the process of hiring someone there to take over the business and was moving back to Dallas. He had met the love of his life and was planning to ask her to marry him.

When Lauren was diagnosed with cancer, Chase was by her side all of the way. When she was in the hospital the first time, I would try to find out what the doctors were saying and doing for her. He made sure that to give me updates and I was amazed how he could tell me the medical terms and then break them down for me. Lauren had been involved with so many different churches with singing and worshiping, and he told me the halls were lined with many ministers praying for her.

He continued to help her and be by her side as much as he could. Like I have said, family was top priority with him. Chase loved the Lord and in his own quiet way, you knew how strong his relationship was. He was trying to change some of his habits as a single man. He wanted to get married and be the kind of husband that he wanted to be. He did not believe in having children and then getting married. He wanted to do the right things that he had been taught.

The tragic night that he was killed, he was talking on the phone with the young lady he was serious about; he was so happy about their future. He hung up the phone. Then a tragic situation came up, the police were called, and we never really found out what happened except that he lost his life that night. Debbie and Con were dealing with Lauren being sick and helping take care of her children so they never pursued what happened.

I cannot explain how much our whole family grieved over his death. A young man of twenty-eight had died. My heart was broken in a million pieces. We went through a memorial service and so many friends comforted us during this time.

Lauren was going through treatment at this time, but she and her cousin planned a beautiful service for Chase. She and Andrew were able to bring Rick Pino and his band to First Assembly and their music was amazing. Andrew and Lauren sang a beautiful duet and you just knew that he would have been pleased. He died and then Lauren died nineteen months later. How in the world can parents go through such a heartbreaking experience as this? Only a *strong faith* can help you day by day.

I would like to tell you that the legacy that Chase left for us is to remember to love your family, love your friends, and most of all *love our God.* I can still hear that little raspy voice saying, "Nana I love you and everything will be all right." It has been five years this past May since he went to Heaven, but he will always be in the midst of our family gatherings and in our hearts.

I guess I will end with this chapter. I have to admit that tears are streaming down my face as I am remembering my two precious grand babies. I can just hear them cheering me on about my book and telling my family stories.

My prayer is that all of these stories will bring you peace, hope, healing, and the will to do what God has called you to do. Do not let the world destroy your faith. Just keep on keeping on and keep the faith.

Sincerely, with all the love in my heart, and may God bless each one of you,

Eleanor Wilbanks

BIBLIOGRAPHY

"A Diamond and a Pearl." Invitation Ministries. Posted March 15, 2022. https://www.invitationministries.com/post/a-diamond-and-a-pearl.

Printed in the United States
by Baker & Taylor Publisher Services